Little
Pebble™

Festivals in Different Cultures

Christmas

Raintree is an imprint of Capstone Global Library Limited, a company incorporated in England and Wales having its registered office at 264 Banbury Road, Oxford, OX2 7DY – Registered company number: 6695582

www.raintree.co.uk
myorders@raintree.co.uk

Edited by Jill Kalz
Designed by Julie Peters
Picture research by Pam Mitsakos
Production by Steve Walker

Printed and bound in India.

ISBN 978 1 4747 3792 0 (hardback)
20 19 18 17 16
10 9 8 7 6 5 4 3 2 1

ISBN 978 1 4747 3798 2 (paperback)
21 20 19 18 17
10 9 8 7 6 5 4 3 2 1

British Library Cataloguing in Publication Data
A full catalogue record for this book is available from the British Library.

Acknowledgements
We would like to thank the following for permission to reproduce photographs: Shutterstock: Alexander Hoffmann, 15, Anneka, 9, Armari36, 7, Dasha Petrenko, 5, debra hughes, design element, Ernest R. Prim, 13, fotohunter, 3, haveseen, 11, Monkey Business Images, 19, Nancy Bauer, 6, oliveromg, 10, Sandra Cunningham, cover, SpeedKingz, 17, StacieStauffSmith Photos, 1, 22, 23, back cover, Timmary, 18, Yuganov Konstantin, 21

Every effort has been made to contact copyright holders of material reproduced in this book. Any omissions will be rectified in subsequent printings if notice is given to the publisher.

All the Internet addresses (URLs) given in this book were valid at the time of going to press. However, due to the dynamic nature of the Internet, some addresses may have changed, or sites may have changed or ceased to exist since publication. While the author and publisher regret any inconvenience this may cause readers, no responsibility for any such changes can be accepted by either the author or the publisher.

Contents

What is Christmas?

Bells ring. Candles glow.

Christmas is coming!

Christmas is the birthday

of Jesus. It is 25th December.

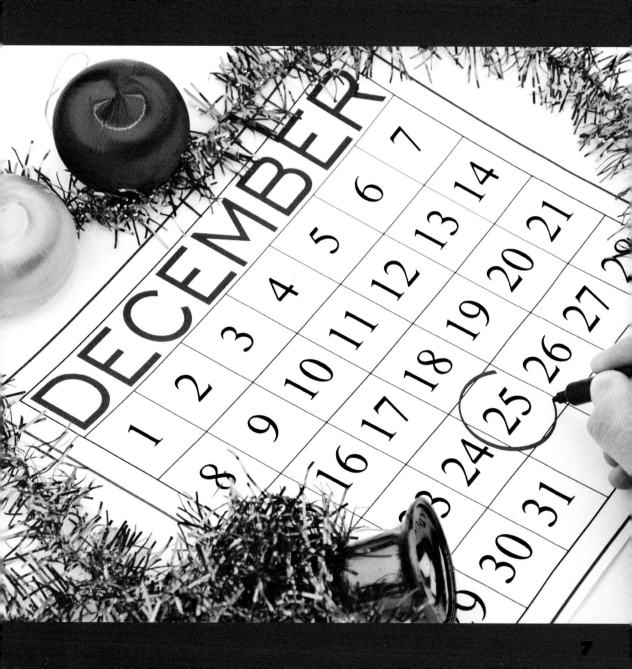

DECEMBER

	1	2	3	4	5	6	7
	8	9	10	11	12	13	14
		16	17	18	19	20	21
		23	24	(25)	26	27	28
		29	30	31			

The Bible says Jesus was
the son of God. Jesus' mother
was Mary. Jesus was born
in a stable.

Getting ready

People send cards to friends.

They make cookies.

Many people put up a tree.
They add lights. They put
a star on top.

See Jesus and his family?

They are out for all to see.

Christmas is here!

Many people go to church.
They sing carols. They share
joy with each other.

Families eat a big dinner.

They tell stories.

They give gifts.

Christmas is a time
of peace and love.
It is a time to share!

Glossary

Bible book written thousands of years ago that is holy to Christians

carol joyful song sung at Christmastime

Christmas Christian holiday; Christians follow the religion of Christianity

stable building where farm animals are kept

Read more

All About Christmas (Celebrate Winter), Martha E. H. Rustad (Raintree, 2016)

Christmas (Holidays and Festivals), Nancy Dickman (Raintree, 2011)

The First Christmas (My Very First Bible Stories), Lois Rock (Lion Hudson, May 2011)

Websites

www.whychristmas.com/cultures/
Learn about Christmas traditions all around the world! Read stories, play games and watch videos all about Christmas.

www.allthingschristmas.com/traditions.html
Learn about different Christmas traditions and how they started. Play games, listen to music, find recipes and more!

Comprehension Questions

1. What is Christmas?

2. Name three things people may do on Christmas.

Index